GW00703483

Mercy: Greatest Gift

Meeting the Love of Christ

by
Barbara Reed Mason

*All booklets are published thanks to the
generous support of the members of the
Catholic Truth Society*

CATHOLIC TRUTH SOCIETY
PUBLISHERS TO THE HOLY SEE

Contents

Introduction 3

Instruct the Ignorant 7

Counsel the Doubtful 21

Admonish Sinners 28

Bear Wrongs Patiently 35

Forgive Offenses Willingly 38

Comfort the Afflicted 42

Pray for the Living and the Dead 48

The Scripture quotes in this pamphlet are from the CTS New Catholic Bible published in 2012 by the Incorporated Catholic Truth Society. All images © Fr Lawrence Lew OP.

All rights reserved. First published 2015 by The Incorporated Catholic Truth Society, 40-46 Harleyford Road London SE11 5AY Tel: 020 7640 0042 Fax: 020 7640 0046. © 2015 The Incorporated Catholic Truth Society.

ISBN 978 1 78469 093 9

Introduction

This is the greatest gift of mercy: bringing people
to Christ and giving them the opportunity to know
and savour his love. (St John Paul II)

Pope Francis has proclaimed an Extraordinary Jubilee
beginning on 8th December 2015 (Feast of the Immaculate
Conception of the Blessed Virgin Mary) and ending on
20th November 2016 (Feast of Christ the King). He wants
this Jubilee to be a Holy Year of Mercy, one that "begins
with a spiritual conversion".[1] For that reason, spiritual
conversion is the aim of this pamphlet, and we will use the
seven Spiritual Works of Mercy to help unlock the process
of conversion.

Many Catholics today seem unaware that the Church
encourages seven Spiritual Works of Mercy to keep the
supernatural life of the Body of Christ vigorous. We seem to
be more familiar with the seven Corporal Works of Mercy:
feed the hungry; give drink to the thirsty; clothe the naked;
shelter the homeless; visit the sick and the imprisoned;
bury the dead. These deeds are easily recognisable as

---

[1] "Dear brothers and sisters, I have often thought about how the Church
might make clear its mission of being a witness to mercy. It is a journey
that begins with a spiritual conversion."

important practical activities. But as Pope Francis has often said, the Church must not be seen as just another NGO (non-governmental organisation), and as one Catholic encyclopedia[2] points out: "it must not be forgotten that the works of mercy demand more than a humanitarian basis if they are to serve as instruments in bringing about our eternal salvation. The proper motive is indispensable and this must be drawn from the supernatural order."

Human beings are more than bodies with rational souls. We are body, soul and spirit, as Pope Benedict XVI explained:

> 'May the God of peace make you perfect and holy; and may you all be kept blameless, spirit, soul and body, for the coming of our Lord Jesus Christ' (*1 Th* 5:23). We are, therefore, spirit, soul and body. We are part of this world, tied to the possibilities of our material condition, while at the same time we are open to an infinite horizon, able to converse with God and to welcome him within us.

God has made human beings in his image and likeness, and he has revealed who he is and why he made us:

> God himself is an eternal exchange of love, Father, Son and Holy Spirit, and he has destined us to share in that exchange. (*Catechism of the Catholic Church* 221)

---

[2] Catholic Online Encyclopedia.

The Spiritual Works of Mercy serve this fundamental reality and underpin the Corporal Works of Mercy. They are:

1. Instruct the ignorant
2. Counsel the doubtful
3. Admonish sinners
4. Bear wrongs patiently
5. Forgive offences willingly
6. Comfort the afflicted
7. Pray for the living and the dead.

Instruct the Ignorant

There is a reason why "instruct the ignorant" is the first Spiritual Work of Mercy we will look at. Sometimes it is expressed "instruct the uninformed". However, if we ourselves are not informed of the basic truths of our existence in Christ, then not only will we be building our house on sand, as Jesus said (cf. *Mt* 7:24-27), but we will be unable to instruct others properly. Our own foundation needs to be solidly based on the truth. And truth is not mere intellectual information - truth is a Person: "I am the Truth," said Jesus! (Cf. *Jn* 14:6). However, the Lord Jesus wants you and me to come to that realisation ourselves, based not only on learning and believing what he said and did, but by personally encountering him. St John Paul II insisted on this point when talking about religious instruction (catechesis):

> Genuine catechesis is not limited to imparting a patrimony of truths, rather it aims at introducing people to a full and conscious life of faith. It is important to proclaim the Gospel as 'news', the '*Good News*', totally centred on the Person of Jesus, the Son of God and Redeemer of man. Catechesis must help people to 'meet' Jesus Christ, to converse with him and to immerse themselves in him. Without the vibrance of

this encounter, Christianity becomes a soulless religious traditionalism which easily yields to the attacks of secularism or the enticements of alternative religious offerings. This encounter then, as experience confirms, is not fostered by dry 'lessons' alone, but rather, so to speak, 'caught' by the power of a living witness. (*L'Osservatore Romano*, 27th September 1999, p. 8)

The *Catechism of the Catholic Church* underlines this exhortation:

The transmission of the Christian faith consists primarily in proclaiming Jesus Christ in order to lead others to faith in him. From the beginning, the first disciples burned with the desire to lead others to proclaim Christ: 'We cannot but speak of what we have seen and heard.' And they invite people of every era to enter into the joy of their communion with Christ. (*CCC* 425)

Pope Benedict XVI and Pope Francis continued their predecessor's emphasis on the encounter with the Person of Jesus:

…we encounter the Lord, not as an idea or a moral proposal but, rather, as a Person who wishes to enter into a relationship with us, who wants to be a friend and to renew our life to make it like his. (Pope Benedict XVI, 4th March 2012)

The joy of the gospel fills the hearts and lives of all who encounter Jesus…I invite all Christians, everywhere, at this very moment, to a renewed personal encounter with Jesus Christ, or at least an openness to letting him encounter them; I ask all of you to do this unfailingly each day. No one should think that this invitation is not meant for him or her, since 'no one is excluded from the joy brought by the Lord'. (Pope Francis, *Evangelii Gaudium* 1, 3)

'Beginning' questions

The popes quoted above have emphasised two words or expressions as fundamental: the *encounter with Jesus* and the proclamation of the *Gospel* (the 'Good News'). Are we able to share our own *encounter with Jesus*, and confidently and joyfully proclaim the *Gospel*? If not, we may be asking "How do we encounter Jesus?" and "What exactly is the Gospel ('Good News')?"

To answer those questions we need to start with two other questions which are even more basic: "Who is God?" and "Can we possibly know for certain that he exists?" Yes, we can know about God and that he exists through our reason, by observing his Creation: "For what can be known about God is perfectly plain to them since God himself has made it plain. Ever since God created the world his everlasting power and deity - however invisible - have been there for the mind to see in the things he has made" (*Rm* 1:20).

Knowing *about* God, however, is not the same as *knowing* him personally. This is what *faith* is: God personally revealing himself to us.

> Faith, in its deepest essence, is the openness of the human heart to the gift: to God's self-revelation in the Holy Spirit. (Pope St John Paul II, *Dominum et Vivificantem* 51)

You and I can learn a lot about an historical person by reading and studying his or her life. We might become so knowledgeable that we are able to deliver an articulate lecture about that person. We might even hold that person in great esteem. But none of those things can compare to actually meeting that person and establishing a relationship with him or her. It is the same with God. Only he knows who he really is, so only he can reveal himself:

> After all, the depths of a man can only be known by his own spirit, not by any other man, and in the same way the depths of God can only be known by the Spirit of God. (*1 Co* 2:11)

God has revealed himself to be totally 'other' than anything we could have known through our own mind:

> Through divine revelation, God chose to communicate himself and the eternal decisions of his will regarding the salvation of men. That is to say, he chose to share

with them those divine treasures which totally transcend the understanding of the human mind. (*Dei Verbum* 6)

So who *does* he say he is, then? God reveals himself to be One eternal Being, but three equal and distinct Persons: Father, Son and Holy Spirit. He gives us a hint of that reality in the first chapter of the Bible (*Gn* 1:26-27) and develops that revelation of himself throughout Scripture (*Mt* 28:19; *Jn* 14:16-17, 15:26, 16:13-15).

The encounter with the Lord

People get to know each other primarily by communicating through words. God communicates with us through his word, but God's Word is a Person, the same creative Word through whom he made everything:

In the beginning was the Word: the Word was with God and the Word was God. He was with God in the beginning. Through him all things came to be, not one thing had its being but through him. (*Jn* 1:1-3)

The sacred Scriptures are a place of encounter with God's Word because "All Scripture is inspired by God" (*2 Tm* 3:16). There is a beautiful invitation in the Church's document on Divine Revelation which should encourage us to open our Bibles expectantly:

In the sacred books, the Father who is in heaven comes lovingly to meet his children and talks with them. (*DV* 21)

Before his death, Jesus prayed to his Father for his disciples: "Consecrate them in the truth; your word is truth" (*Jn* 17:17). This word is also a divine and creative word which can have a life-changing effect:

> The word of God is something alive and active: it cuts like any double-edged sword but more finely: it can slip through the place where the soul is divided from the spirit, or joints from the marrow; it can judge the secret emotions and thoughts. (*Heb* 4:12)

Do you remember the story of St Augustine's conversion which he recounted in his *Confessions*? Augustine lived his life seeking self-indulgence in every way, but he wasn't finding the answers to his deepest longings. One day he picked up a Bible after hearing what seemed to him to be a child's voice saying, "Pick up and read!" He opened it and his eyes lit on a verse which pierced his very being. It wasn't just a beautiful phrase that appealed to his intellect or senses. No, he knew that he was being spoken to directly by the Word himself who clearly knew him through and through and was challenging him to change his life. It was his first personal encounter with the living word of the Lord and he was overwhelmed. We all know his famous prayer: "O Lord! Our hearts are restless until they rest in you!"

To come to Jesus our *hearts* must be open, not only our minds. The word 'heart' in a biblical context means our 'innermost being' where we choose for or against God. It is the Holy Spirit "who moves the heart and converts it to God, who opens the eyes of the mind and makes it easy for all to accept and believe the truth" (*DV* 5). The Holy Spirit leads us to Jesus who assured us: "But when the Spirit of truth comes he will lead you to the complete truth…he will glorify me" (*Jn* 16:13,14). And again:

"When the Advocate comes, whom I shall send you from the Father, the Spirit of truth who issues from the Father, he will be my witness." (*Jn* 15:26)

We can also encounter the Lord in personal and community prayer; therefore, neglecting prayer - both private and communal - prevents this possibility. And of course, we meet the Lord in the sacraments - but again, only if we are open to that encounter and if we are 'well-disposed'. Jesus is always present in the sacraments, but are we present to him? The following well-known prayer can help us:

Come Holy Spirit, fill the hearts of your faithful and enkindle in us the fire of your love!

The Gospel

The word 'Gospel' means 'Good News', and it really is Good News because now every human being has the option to live forever in the fullness of love.

In the beginning of the history of man, *living forever,* in the fullness of love, was a 'given', not an option. Why? Because the first human beings were in union with God, who himself is Love and Eternal Life, and "as long as he remained in the divine intimacy, man would not have to suffer or die" (*CCC* 376).

> The first man was not only created good, but was also established in friendship with his Creator and in harmony with himself and all creation around him... this grace of original holiness was 'to share in divine life'. (*CCC* 374, 375)

The first human beings personally experienced the loving plan of God which was mentioned in the Introduction to this booklet: "God himself is an eternal exchange of love, Father, Son and Holy Spirit, and he has destined us to share in that exchange" (*CCC* 221).

But even though our first parents knew God intimately and shared his divine life, they chose to separate themselves from him, thereby separating themselves from divine Wisdom, perfect Love and everlasting Life. By this choice they reduced themselves to "a lower, incomplete state":[3] their minds were darkened without divine Wisdom, they were spiritually dead because they were deprived of the Holy Spirit who is "the giver of life", and they became centred on themselves instead of God. Why did they do this?

They chose to believe the devil, who was originally created by God as the Archangel Lucifer but later rebelled against God and was thrown down to earth (cf. *Rv* 12:7-9).

---

[3] *Gaudium et Spes* 13.

The devil planted a seed of suspicion in the mind of man that God would limit him instead of being the source of his freedom. This is what the parable of the Garden of Eden is all about: it is a "symbolic narrative" (as St John Paul II called it) using figurative language to explain a deep and primeval event that occurred at the beginning of the history of man (cf. *CCC* 390).

When Adam (meaning "the Man") and Eve (meaning "the mother of all the living") gave their allegiance to the words of Satan and scorned the Word of God, they not only separated themselves from God, but they gave the devil a certain domination over them:

> By our first parents' sin, the devil has acquired a certain domination over man, even though man remains free. Original sin 'entails captivity under the power of him who thenceforth had the power of death, that is, the devil'. (*CCC* 407)

This is why Jesus referred to the devil as "the prince of this world" (*Jn* 12:31), and Scripture says that "the whole world lies in the power of the Evil One" (*1 Jn* 5:19).

> God did make man imperishable, he made him in the image of his own nature; it was the devil's envy that brought death into the world (*Ws* 2:23-24a).

So, the human being, whom God created to be his child to *share his very life*, to *rule over all creation*, and to *live forever*, was now subject to death under the captivity of the devil. And even worse, this catastrophic condition of our first parents was passed on to all future generations.

> How did the sin of Adam become the sin of all his descendants? …By yielding to the tempter, Adam and Eve committed a *personal sin*, but this sin affected *the human nature* that they would then transmit in *a fallen state*…a human nature deprived of original holiness (*CCC* 404).

The Church has given us a very good description of the human being in this incomplete state:

> Scripture portrays the tragic consequences of this first disobedience. Adam and Eve immediately lose the grace of original holiness. They become afraid of the God of whom they have conceived a distorted image… The harmony in which they found themselves, thanks to original justice, is now destroyed: the control of the soul's spiritual faculties over the body is shattered; the union of man and woman becomes subject to tensions, their relations henceforth marked by lust and domination. Harmony with creation is broken; visible creation has now become alien and hostile to man… Finally, death makes its entrance into human history. (*CCC* 399, 400)

How can the human being who is now in a state of spiritual death restore himself to eternal life? How can he rescue himself from the tyranny of sin and the devil? How can he reunite himself with the Trinitarian God? The answer is, he cannot.

But God the Father could not stop loving his separated children, so out of his great mercy he sent his Son, the Word through whom everything was made, to rescue humanity and restore us to our dignity as sons and daughters of God. The Word of God became man and lived every aspect of human existence, from the womb to physical death, overturning our rebellion by his faithful obedience to the Father's will. He was tempted in every way that we are, but did not sin (cf. *Heb* 4:15b).

Who is this man who is also the Word of God? His name is Jesus, which means 'God saves'. Jesus saved us by taking upon himself all the sins of mankind and dying on the cross. This was predicted in the books of the Old Testament, and five hundred years before the death of Christ Jesus the prophet Isaiah wrote:

> Yet he was pierced through for our faults, crushed for our sins. On him lies a punishment that brings us peace, and through his wounds we are healed. We had all gone astray like sheep, each taking his own way, and the Lord burdened him with the sins of us all. (*Is* 53:5-6)

The Church teaches us:

> Man's sins, following on original sin, are punishable by death (cf. *Rm* 5:12; *1 Co* 15:56). By sending his own Son in the form of...fallen humanity, on account of sin,

God 'made him to be sin who knew no sin, so that in him we might become the righteousness of God'. (*CCC* 602)

Christ died for all men without exception: "There is not, never has been, and never will be a single human being for whom Christ did not suffer". (*CCC* 605)

But his death on the cross was not the end. Jesus, who is fully man, is also fully God, Eternal Life who cannot die. Jesus rose from the dead in his humanity and will die no more. He conquered sin, Satan and death so he made it possible for fallen man to be restored to union with the Trinitarian God, raised up to a *new* and *everlasting* life. Jesus is the "New Adam", the head of a new creation. Anyone who is united to the Resurrected Jesus will also live forever.

And for anyone who is in Christ there is a new creation; the old creation is gone, and now a new one is here. (*2 Co* 5:17)

How does this happen? Through faith and Baptism. "Faith is a personal encounter with Jesus Christ, making oneself a disciple of his" (*General Catechetical Directory* 53). Baptism removes original sin and restores us to life in the Trinity. Pope Francis tells us about the new life after Baptism:

To be born from on high, to be born of the Spirit…is the new life we received in Baptism but which we must develop…we must do our utmost to ensure that this life develops into new life…It is a journey, an arduous journey we must toil to achieve. Yet it does not only depend on us…it depends mainly on the Spirit so that he creates this new life within us.[4]

After his Resurrection and before he ascended to heaven Jesus told his disciples to wait "for what the Father had promised": "It is," he had said, "what you have heard me speak about: John baptised with water but you, not many days from now, will be baptised with the Holy Spirit…you will receive power when the Holy Spirit comes on you, and then you will be my witnesses" (*Ac* 1:4, 5, 8).

The new life which we receive in Baptism is meant to be ongoing and *lived in the power of the Holy Spirit*, not merely through our own strength or willpower. Sometimes even religious people seem unaware of this essential reality. One often gets the impression that some of the baptised believe not only that they can live their Christian life in their own power, but that they can 'earn' their salvation by their good deeds! Of course we must perform good works - we are required to do so - but it is only the grace of God and the gift of the Holy Spirit that gives us *new life* in him:

Because it is by grace that you have been saved, through faith; not by anything of your own, but by a gift from

---

[4] Pope Francis, morning meditation in the chapel of Domus Sanctae Martae, Tuesday, 9th April 2013 (*L'Osservatore Romano*, weekly ed. in English, n. 16, 17th April 2013).

God; not by anything that you have done, so that nobody can claim the credit. (*Ep* 2:8-9)

Those who experience this new life in the Spirit are able to "instruct the ignorant" because they rely not on their human resources alone, but on the spiritual gifts and graces freely given by God to those who believe. Let us have a look at some of these spiritual gifts.

Counsel the Doubtful

At our Baptism the Holy Spirit infused into us seven supernatural gifts called "Sanctifying Gifts", which are strengthened in the Sacrament of Confirmation. Pope Francis explained these gifts in a series of General Audiences.[5] One of these spiritual gifts of the Holy Spirit is the gift of counsel:

> Now, through the gift of counsel, it is God himself, through his Spirit, who enlightens our heart so as to make us understand the right way to speak and to behave and the way to follow. But how does this gift work in us? When we receive and welcome him into our heart, the Holy Spirit immediately begins to make us sensitive to his voice and to guide our thoughts, our feelings and our intentions according to the heart of God. At the same time, he leads us more and more to turn our interior gaze to Jesus, as the model of our way of acting and of relating with God the Father and with the brethren. Counsel, then, is the gift through which the Holy Spirit *enables our conscience to make*

[5] Beginning on 9th April 2014, and continuing from 30th April onwards, Pope Francis gave a series of talks on the seven Sanctifying Gifts of the Holy Spirit in his General Audiences.

a concrete choice in communion with God, according to the logic of Jesus and his Gospel. In this way, the Spirit makes us grow interiorly…he helps us not to fall prey to self-centredness and one's own way of seeing things. The essential condition for preserving this gift is prayer….To pray with the prayers that we all learned as children, but also to pray in our own words. To ask the Lord: 'Lord, help me, give me counsel, what must I do now?' And through prayer we make space so that the Spirit may come and help us in that moment, that he may counsel us on what we all must do. Prayer! Never forget prayer. Never! No one, no one realises when we pray on the bus, on the road: we pray in the silence of our heart. Let us take advantage of these moments to pray, pray that the Spirit give us the gift of counsel.

This supernatural gift of counsel is not only for our own use, it also enables us to *counsel the doubtful*, which our own experience of faith supports (faith here meaning the "personal encounter with Jesus Christ, making ourselves a disciple of his", *GCD* 53). By sharing with another how we 'met' Jesus, or how the Holy Spirit has helped us, we put flesh on the bones of doctrine. A person does not have to have lengthy theological training for this!

I remember when I was teaching in a Catholic high school and one of the older boys approached me to announce that he didn't believe in God. I told him I was sorry to hear it, but wondered why he wanted me to know this. Was he hoping I would try to prove him wrong? So I asked him a question: "What did you have for breakfast today?" He gave me a detailed description. When I enquired whether anyone was with him at the time he said no. "Well, prove it to me," I replied. He was silent. "That's what it's like with me and God," I said. "You can line up a hundred theologians to argue with me but I know whom I have tasted. Like the Psalm says: *Taste and see that the Lord is good* (*Ps* 33[34]:9), which is figurative language for 'know by experience'. As for your opinion of me and what I have just said, you must do what Jesus advised when he said that we could know a tree by its fruit (cf. *Mt* 12:33)."

God himself is Truth, so he cannot lie. Holy Mother Church counsels us: "What moves us to believe is not the fact that revealed truths appear as true and intelligible in the light of our natural reason: we believe 'because of the authority of God himself who reveals them, who can neither deceive nor be deceived'" (*CCC* 156).

Faith is *certain*. It is more certain than all human knowledge because it is founded on the very word of God who cannot lie. To be sure, revealed truths can seem obscure to human reason and experience, but 'the certainty that the divine light gives is greater than that which the light of natural reason gives.' 'Ten thousand difficulties do not make one doubt.' (*CCC* 157)

The love of God which has been poured into our hearts by the Holy Spirit (cf. *Rm* 5:5), and the certainty we have of who he is because we have 'tasted' him and seen that he is good, helps us to choose to believe his word wholeheartedly, as Peter did when the Lord Jesus asked his close disciples if they too would leave with the many who refused to accept his teaching about the Eucharist. Peter replied: "Lord, who shall we go to? You have the message of eternal life, and we believe; we know that you are the Holy One of God" (*Jn* 6:68-69).

Doubts do not always have to be a cause of concern: sometimes they are opportunities to turn to the Lord in a more honest way, thereby allowing him to speak to us in the depths of our spirit and bring us into a deeper relationship with him. Doubts can also move us to rely more on the sanctifying gifts he has already given us, such as the gifts of wisdom and understanding which Pope Francis also explained:

> The first gift of the Holy Spirit…is *wisdom*. But it is not simply human wisdom, which is the fruit of knowledge and experience. …wisdom is precisely this: it is the grace of being able *to see everything with the eyes of God*. …Sometimes we see things according to our liking or according to the condition of our heart, with love or with hate, with envy… No, this is not God's perspective. Wisdom is what the Holy Spirit works

in us so as to enable us to see things with the eyes of God. ...And obviously this comes from *intimacy with God*, from the intimate relationship we have with God, from the relationship children have with their Father. ... The Holy Spirit thus makes the Christian 'wise'. Not in the sense that he has an answer for everything, that he knows everything, but in the sense that he 'knows' about God, he knows how God acts, he knows when something is of God and when it is not of God; he has this wisdom which God places in our hearts. ...And this is something that we cannot invent, that we cannot obtain by ourselves: it is a gift that God gives to those who make themselves docile to the Holy Spirit...and we can all have it. We only have to ask it of the Holy Spirit.[6]

The second gift [is] understanding. We are not dealing here with human understanding, with the intellectual prowess with which we may be more or less endowed. Rather, it is a grace which only the Holy Spirit can infuse and which awakens in a Christian the ability to go beyond the outward appearance of reality and *to probe the depths of the thoughts of God and his plan of salvation*. This of course does not mean that a Christian can comprehend all things and have full knowledge of the designs of God: all of this waits to be revealed in all its clarity once we stand in the sight of God and are

---

[6] Ibid

truly one with Him. However, as the very word suggests, understanding allows us to '*intus legere*', or 'to read inwardly': this gift enables us to understand things as God understands them, with the mind of God. For one can understand a situation with human understanding, with prudence, and this is good. But to understand a situation in depth, as God understands it, is the effect of this gift. …It is clear then that the gift of understanding is *closely connected to faith*. When the Holy Spirit dwells in our hearts and enlightens our minds, he makes us grow day by day in the *understanding of what the Lord has said and accomplished*. Jesus himself told his disciples: I will send you the Holy Spirit and he will enable you to understand all that I have taught you. …And this is what the Holy Spirit does with us: he opens our minds, he opens us to understand better, to understand better the things of God, human beings, situations, all things. The gift of understanding is important for our Christian life.[7]

God wants everyone to reach full knowledge of the truth (cf. *1 Tm* 2:4), because, as Jesus said, "the truth will make you free" (*Jn* 8:32b). To counsel people who are doubtful is a great act of charity, especially if we help them root themselves more deeply in the Word of God, in the graces and gifts of their Baptism and Confirmation, and in their relationship with the Lord Jesus.

---

[7] Ibid

Admonish Sinners

A more modern translation would probably be 'correct sinners', but even that expression doesn't go down well with most people. The motive behind admonishment/ correction *must* be love: love for the person who is in error and concern for their eternal welfare.

By love, of course, is meant the theological virtue of charity. At Baptism, the three theological virtues of faith, hope and charity "are infused by God into the souls of the faithful to make them capable of acting as his children" (*CCC* 1813). This virtue, charity, enables us to "love God above all things for his own sake, and our neighbour as ourselves for the love of God" (*CCC* 1822).

> Charity upholds and purifies our human ability to love, and raises it to the perfection of divine love. (*CCC* 1827)

The *Catechism* teaches that "charity demands beneficence [kindness, charitable acts] and *fraternal correction*" (1829). Fraternal correction is based on the words and actions of God himself who loves us with an everlasting love and does not want us to experience eternal separation from him: he wants "everyone to be saved" (*1 Tm* 2:4).

Have you ever noticed that four times in the Book of Revelation the expression "the second death" is used (*Rv*

2:11; 20:6; 20:14; 21:8)? The "second death" refers to *eternal* death where sinners receive their final punishment. Recall the earlier account of the fall of man from grace - that is, the free choice of the first human beings to separate themselves from life in God, who is Eternal Life. They experienced "death of the soul" (spiritual death),[8] which we have all inherited. We are all born spiritually dead and we can only be brought back to Eternal Life through *faith* in our Lord and Saviour Jesus who died to bring us new life, and *baptism* into that new life (i.e., being re-born spiritually). If we do not personally accept the new Eternal Life which has been won for us, or continue living that new life in Christ, we are in a state of spiritual death, so if we physically die in that condition, our separation from God is eternalised. That is the "second death".

Faith must grow after Baptism and we need to remain in union with Jesus throughout our lives, living for *him* and not ourselves. Unfortunately, the general consensus seems to be that if we are nice people we will somehow 'get to heaven'; it is as if Jesus - and what he did for us by his death on the cross - is irrelevant or optional. But what is *heaven*? Let's look at the following definitions from two popes:

> Revelation teaches us that Heaven is not an abstraction or a place in the clouds, but a living personal relationship of union with the Holy Trinity. (St John Paul II)

---

[8] St Thomas Aquinas: "Sin is the spiritual death of the soul"; cf. *CCC* 403.

> This word *heaven* does not indicate a place above
> the stars but something far more daring and sublime:
> it indicates Christ himself, the divine person who
> welcomes humanity fully and forever, the One in whom
> God and man are inseparably united forever. Man's
> being in God, this is heaven. And we draw close to
> heaven, indeed we enter heaven to the extent we draw
> close to Jesus and enter into communion with him.
> (Pope Benedict XVI)

Charity impels us to "admonish sinners" when it is clear
by their words and deeds that they have rejected their
Baptism. We want them to experience "life to the full" (cf.
Jn 10:10) which Jesus offers us: the new life in the Spirit
which begins now.

Practicalities

How should we admonish sinners? First of all with a motive
of love; and secondly, with an acute awareness of our own
sinfulness, which includes gratitude to the Lord for rescuing
us and restoring us to himself out of sheer mercy. And
thirdly, praying first for the gift of counsel for ourselves!

I was once told in the Sacrament of Reconciliation that if
I had to correct someone I should first pray that the person
being corrected "would hear the love of the Lord" through
my words. Of course, sometimes their initial reaction
seemed to indicate that my prayer wasn't answered! But
experience has shown that in many cases the person had an

open heart because they eventually perceived his love and responded to the Lord.

Normally it is best if we already have a natural relationship with the person we are admonishing, meaning that we know them personally and they are aware of our love and respect for them. Scripture gives some advice on how to approach different people, in the pastoral letter of St Paul to Timothy:

> Do not speak harshly to a man older than yourself, but advise him as you would your own father; treat the younger men as brothers and older women as you would your mother. Always treat young women with propriety, as if they were sisters. (*1 Tm* 5:1-2)

Correcting others can also depend on whether or not we are in a position of authority, for example a priest, a parent or a teacher: all cases in which we are bound to exercise our God-given responsibility. Scripture gives examples of public correction which is necessary to prevent confusion, especially when the wrongdoer has spiritual authority, such as the time when Paul confronted Peter (*Ga* 2:11ff), or the instructions for bishops on admonishment (*1 Tm* 5:20; *Ti* 1:9,11,13).

Not judging

In Baptism we have all been anointed "priest, prophet and king", so when the Lord speaks to his prophets in the

Scriptures we can take it that he is speaking to us. For example, the Lord says:

> If I say to a wicked man: Wicked wretch, you are to die, and you do not speak to warn the wicked man to renounce his ways, then he shall die for his sin, but I will hold you responsible for his death. If, however, you do warn a wicked man to renounce his ways and repent, and he does not repent, then he shall die for his sin, but you yourself will have saved your life. (*Ezk* 33:8-9)

The Lord also says: "What! Am I likely to take pleasure in the death of a wicked man - it is the Lord who speaks - and not prefer to see him renounce his wickedness and live?" (*Ezk* 18:23).

The word "wicked" jars for some in this current climate. The problem is that most people do not differentiate between the sin and the sinner. God hates our sin because it separates us from life in him (which makes it "wicked"), but he can never stop loving each one of us with perfect love. He always loves *us*, but he would deny who he is if he always loved what we *do*, especially if it harms us and others and prevents us from experiencing our dignity as his sons and daughters.

"Do not judge and you will not be judged," said Jesus (*Mt* 7:1). People tend to remember the scene with the woman caught in adultery and the Lord's words to her when she was accused of that sin: "Neither do I condemn you," he said; but his next words are frequently forgotten: "Don't sin anymore" (*Jn* 8:11).

The Lord also called people "hypocrites" when they noticed the splinter in someone's eye while they had a wooden beam in their own (cf. *Mt* 7: 3ff). But he never said not to remove the splinter in the other's eye: quite the contrary! "Take the plank out of your own eye first, and then you will see clearly enough to take the splinter out of your brother's eye." In other words, be conscious of the fact that "there but for the grace of God go I", but do help rescue your brother or sister. One biblical footnote on these verses explains: "This is not a prohibition against recognising the faults of others…but in passing judgement in a spirit of arrogance, forgetful of one's faults" (*New American Bible*).

Correcting our brother or sister

The Word of God speaks to each one of us: "Brothers, if one of you misbehaves, the more spiritual of you who set him right should do so in a spirit of gentleness, not forgetting that you may be tempted yourselves" (*Ga* 6:1).

"If your brother does something wrong, go and have it out with him alone, between your two selves. If he listens to you, you have won back your brother. If he does not listen, take one or two others along with you: the evidence of two or three witnesses is required to sustain any charge." (*Mt* 18:15-16)

[A servant of the Lord] has to be gentle when he corrects people who dispute what he says, never forgetting that God may give them a change of mind so that they recognise the truth and come to their senses, once out of the trap where the devil caught them and kept them enslaved. (*2 Tm* 2:25-26)

And finally:

My brothers, if one of you strays away from the truth, and another brings him back to it, he may be sure that anyone who can bring back a sinner from the wrong way that he has taken will be saving a soul from death and covering up a great number of sins. (*Jm* 5:19-20)

Bear Wrongs Patiently

Some sources express this spiritual work of mercy as, "Be patient with those in error", which puts a slightly different slant on things. First of all, let's read the Word of God which, as always, throws light on reality:

> An unspiritual person is one who does not accept anything of the Spirit of God: he sees it all as nonsense; it is beyond his understanding because it can only be understood by means of the Spirit. (*1 Co* 2:14)

The "unspiritual person" is described further: "Intellectually they are in the dark, and they are estranged from the life of God, without knowledge because they have shut their hearts to it" (*Ep* 4:18).

As we have already mentioned, God desires everyone to be saved and to come to the knowledge of the truth! (Cf. *1 Tm* 2:4.) So how does that work when we come up against an "unspiritual person"? God is patient with us, so as his children we are asked to show the same mercy toward others. His grace working through us as we practise this particular spiritual work of mercy has a supernatural power to "set the captives free". Take the example of Cardinal Nguyen Van Thuan, kept imprisoned in solitary confinement for years by atheistic Communists.

He preached the Good News of Jesus through his non-retaliation, and by "bearing wrongs patiently" brought his captors to conversion and the Word of the Lord was fulfilled: "Erring spirits will learn wisdom and murmurers accept instruction" (*Is* 29:24).

But it is not only those in error with whom we must patiently bear wrongs: often it is our brothers and sisters in Christ, or our own relatives, who 'wrong' us. What then? The saints show us what to do, such as Catherine of Siena whose mother was so irritated by Catherine's devotion to prayer that she gave her innumerable tasks to accomplish in the home, thereby leaving Catherine no time to escape to her room to be with the Lord. Catherine responded by telling the Lord that she could still visit him in the "room" of her heart. When her siblings ridiculed her for her religious beliefs and practices she decided to pretend they were the Apostles, and served them at table with a humble and reverent attitude.

Scripture gives us some advice about bearing wrongs patiently:

> Slaves must be respectful and obedient to their masters, not only when they are kind and gentle but also when they are unfair. You see, there is some merit in putting up with the pains of unearned punishment if it is done for the sake of God but there is nothing meritorious in taking a beating patiently if you have done something

wrong to deserve it. The merit, in the sight of God, is in bearing it patiently when you are punished after doing your duty.

This, in fact, is what you were called to do, because Christ suffered for you and left an example for you to follow the way he took. He had not done anything wrong, and "there had been no perjury in his mouth" [*Is* 53:7,9]. He was insulted and did not retaliate with insults; when he was tortured he made no threats but he put his trust in the righteous judge. (*1 P* 2:18-23)

We are meant to *share* Christ's life, not merely imitate it from the outside, and that includes sharing his suffering. How else can we be formed into his image except by undergoing the same things he went through? It is a privilege when he allows us to experience what he experienced. St Francis explained that truth to his brother friars when he asked them what they thought would give them the most joy. They had lots of ideas but Francis's answer surprised them: "Rejection!" he exclaimed, because that was the most common experience of Jesus (and still is!). If he allows us to suffer rejection *because of our union with him*, we really are privy to his life.

Forgive Offences Willingly

Jesus said: "If your brother does something wrong, reprove him and, if he is sorry, forgive him. And if he wrongs you seven times a day and seven times comes back to you and says, 'I am sorry', you must forgive him" (*Lk* 17:3-4).

Oh my! *Who* can do *that*? Does Jesus know about the alcoholic husband who continues to break his promise not to have another drop? Or the work colleague who slanders you again and again in the office even after she apologises? Or any other heinous wrongdoing one can imagine? Yes, he does. In fact he knows about it all even better than we do, because he forgives *us* again and again and again.

Despite what it seems, Jesus is not trying to lay a heavy burden on us by giving us the command to forgive. After all, he told us that his yoke is easy and his burden light (cf. *Mt* 11:30). Why would he say that? Because he carries our burden with us, and assists us with his *grace*.

Does this sound too 'super-spiritual' and out of touch for the average baptised person? The *Catechism*, which Pope St John Paul II called "a sure norm for teaching the faith", reveals how well Holy Mother Church knows her children:

> It is not in our power not to feel, or to forget, an offence. (*CCC* 2843)

Well, then, how are we meant to comply with the Lord's command to forgive if it is impossible for us? The *Catechism* continues:

> …but the heart that offers itself to the Holy Spirit turns injury into compassion and purifies the memory in transforming the hurt into intercession. (*CCC* 2843)

We need to turn our hearts to the Holy Spirit and ask him to do what we cannot do - or may not even *want* to do. Initially we may only be able to pray: "Lord, I know I am supposed to forgive but at this moment I am not able to, nor do I even want to forgive! Please give me the *desire* to forgive in the first place, then help me pray for the one I cannot forgive." By doing this, we allow the Holy Spirit to really get to work in our hearts, and as the *Catechism* states, he will turn the injury into compassion, and eventually even purify our memories! Now that is miraculous!

I know a woman whose husband ran off with her best friend. It was the cause of her turning to the Lord in a deeper way, and she surrendered her life into his hands. Several years later she spoke up at a prayer meeting in our parish. "Do you see these earrings?" She touched her ears. "They were a birthday gift years ago from my best friend who later took away my husband. This is the first time I have worn them since then. Tonight I put them on happily and with no malice. The Holy Spirit has set me free!"

Clearly our vocation to live as children of God and disciples of Jesus is supernatural: it requires *grace*. What is that?

> Grace is a *participation in the life of God*. It introduces us into the intimacy of Trinitarian life: by Baptism the Christian participates in the grace of Christ...he receives the life of the Spirit who breathes charity into him. (*CCC* 1997)

Participation in God's life is the key:

> It is impossible to keep the Lord's commandment by imitating the divine model from the outside; there has to be a vital participation, coming from the depths of the heart, in the holiness and the mercy and the love of our God. Only the Spirit by whom we live can make 'ours' the same mind that was in Christ Jesus. (*CCC* 2842)

Once again we recall that God's plan for his children is to share his divine life - beginning now, with Baptism, and continuing until we meet him face to face. But God's free initiative demands man's free response:

> God has created man in his image by conferring on him, along with freedom, the power to know him and love him. The soul only enters *freely* into the communion of love. (*CCC* 2002)

Do we freely want to live in union with God and share his divine compassion and mercy, for his sake, for our sake, and for the good of our world?

Prayer of Surrender to Jesus

Lord Jesus, I confess that I am a sinner.
I know that you want to cleanse me of
all sin and give me new life in you.
I believe that you died for me. Please
forgive me and restore in me the graces
and gifts you gave me in my baptism.
I surrender my life to you and ask you
to be my Lord. Come into my heart
and help me respond to your love.
Thank you, Lord Jesus. Amen.

Comfort the Afflicted

What is meant by "the afflicted": anyone who is any pain, suffering or distress. We are asked to comfort the sorrowful! But remember this is a *spiritual work of mercy*, not merely temporary relief. By a *spiritual work* we do not mean offering pious platitudes. God's comfort is a reality.

Perhaps a personal example might help explain this truth. When my husband and I lived in the Republic of Panama there was a leper colony just outside Panama City. One of the priests in our parish used to celebrate Mass once a month for the few lepers who still lived there and one day he asked if anyone could accompany him because he was delivering fruit and vegetables donated by some of the villagers nearby and he needed some help. I went along and met three of the lepers who were Catholics. They expressed a wish to go to Mass more often so my husband and I would regularly drive through the jungle road, pick them up, and take them to Sunday Mass in our parish.

In our conversations with Richard and Ruth (a married couple) and Lopez (the third leper) it was obvious that, although they were being provided with food and other material necessities, they were not being fed spiritually other than the weekly Eucharist, so I began lending them taped talks by priests and others to listen to during the

week. During this time, the United States put economic sanctions on Panama because of the dictator in power, General Noriega. This meant that Panama could no longer get its medical supplies from the USA, so the medication for the leper colony became out of date. Not only that, the money was no longer available for full-time carers, and the one remaining nurse could come only once every twenty-four hours to give the lepers a hot drink and a meal. (They had no fingers, of course, so could not cook for themselves or even boil a kettle.)

One evening I collected Ruth to take her to a prayer meeting in our parish. She told me that she thought Lopez had 'lost it', because the day before when the nurse came to prepare their one meal, he was sitting on a bench in the garden listening to one of the taped talks by a priest on the Eucharist, and when she called him to come and eat, he remained on the bench listening to the tape. She couldn't understand it! But I had come to know Lopez, who, despite his disease, disfigurement, and isolation in that leper colony, had a total lack of bitterness and a wonderful sense of humour, and clearly, a love for the Lord. He was mesmerised by the priest's talk on the Bread of Life. The spiritual food he was receiving comforted him far more than the hot meal he was offered.

We need to give true comfort, based in reality, based on the sanctifying gift of piety. Let's turn to Pope Francis for an explanation of this gift:

Today we want to pause on a gift of the Holy Spirit which is often misunderstood and considered in a superficial way; instead it touches the heart of our identity and our Christian life: it is the gift of piety.

It is necessary to clarify immediately that this gift is not identified with having compassion for someone, having pity for one's neighbour, but it indicates our belonging to God and our profound bond with Him, a bond that gives meaning to the whole of our life and which keeps us firm, in communion with Him, also in the most difficult and trying moments.

1. This bond with the Lord is not intended as a duty or an imposition. It is a bond that comes from within. It is a relation lived with the heart: it is our friendship with God, given us by Jesus; a friendship that changes our life and fills us with enthusiasm and joy. Therefore, the gift of piety arouses in us, first of all, gratitude and praise…Piety, therefore, is a synonym of authentic religious spirit, of filial confidence in God, of that capacity to pray to Him with love and simplicity which is proper of persons who are humble of heart.

2. If the gift of piety makes us grow in our relation and communion with God and leads us to live as His children, at the same time it helps us to pour this love also on others and to recognise them as brothers. And then, yes, we will be moved by sentiments of piety - not

of pietism! - in our dealings with those around us and those we meet every day. Why do I say not pietism?

Because some think that to have piety is to close one's eyes, to make an imaginary face, and feign to be like a saint. …This isn't the gift of piety. The gift of piety means to be truly capable of rejoicing with those in joy, to weep with those who weep, to welcome and help those who are in need. There is a very close relation between the gift of piety and meekness. The gift of piety that the Holy Spirit gives us makes us meek, it makes us tranquil, patient, in peace with God, and at the service of others with meekness. …May the Holy Spirit give all of us this gift of piety.[9]

St Paul clearly understood how to comfort the afflicted as a spiritual work of mercy:

Blessed be the God and Father of our Lord Jesus Christ, a gentle Father and the God of all consolation, who comforts us in all our sorrows, so that we can offer others, in their sorrows, the consolation we have received from God ourselves. Indeed, as the sufferings of Christ overflow to us, so, through Christ, does our consolation overflow. When we are made to suffer, it is for your consolation and salvation. When, instead,

---

[9] Beginning on 9th April 2014, and continuing from 30th April onwards, Pope Francis gave a series of talks on the seven Sanctifying Gifts of the Holy Spirit in his General Audiences.

we are comforted, this should be a consolation to you, supporting you in patiently bearing the same sufferings as we bear. And our hope for you is confident, since we know that, sharing our sufferings, you will also share our consolations. (*2 Co* 1:3-7)

In this exhortation St Paul makes it clear that it is God who is the source of all comfort, but that we as the Body of Christ need to share God's comfort with each other, especially as there will be times when some are in distress and others are not.

Pray for the Living and the Dead

This is the final Spiritual Work of Mercy, which may seem to be the least practical or 'hands on' of all the spiritual works. But it is a work of mercy that can be done by anyone of any age, whether healthy or ill, mobile or immobile, and as Pope Francis said, we can pray always and anywhere. It is probably the most humble of all the works: no one knows you are praying except God, and the answers to the prayers can only be attributed to him.

Some may wonder why we pray for the dead since they have already left this earth. Remember, though, that they still exist, and there is no time with God. God is eternal, the everlasting 'now'. So even if someone has already died, our prayer can be applied to them.

> But there is one thing, my friends, that you must never forget: that with the Lord, a 'day' can mean a thousand years, and a thousand years is like a day. (*2 P* 3:8)

> To your eyes a thousand years are like yesterday, come and gone, no more than a watch in the night. (*Ps* 89[90]:4)

We pray for the dead because we do not know the state of anyone's soul when they die. Holy Mother Church gives us hope through the doctrine on Purgatory:

All who die in God's grace and friendship, but still imperfectly purified, are indeed assured of their eternal salvation; but after death they undergo purification, so as to achieve the holiness necessary to enter the joy of heaven. …The Church gives the name Purgatory to this final purification of the elect. (*CCC* 1030, 1031)

Mass offered for the dead is particularly powerful, as is participating in a funeral Mass:

The Eucharist is the heart of the Paschal reality of Christian death. In the Eucharist, the Church expresses her efficacious communion with the departed: offering to the Father in the Holy Spirit the sacrifice of the death and Resurrection of Christ, she asks him to purify his child of his sins and their consequences…It is by the Eucharist thus celebrated that the community of the faithful, especially the family of the deceased, learn to live in communion with the one who 'has fallen asleep in the Lord', by communicating in the Body of Christ of which he is a living member and, then, by praying for him and with him. (*CCC* 1689)

Praying for others shows both our love and our inter-dependence. Everyone needs to be spiritually supported by prayer, and it is a great comfort to know that our brothers and sisters in the Body of Christ are praying for us. St Francis Xavier attributed all his many baptisms to the prayers of the Carmelite nuns who interceded for

him and his mission, knowing that their prayers were the 'powerhouse' behind his spiritual activities. St Thérèse of Lisieux, who never left her convent, was named Patron Saint of Missionaries because of her fervent prayer for the salvation of souls.

> The great men and women of God were great intercessors. Intercession is like a 'leaven' in the heart of the Trinity. It is a way of penetrating the Father's heart and discovering new dimensions which can shed light on concrete situations and change them. We can say that God's heart is touched by our intercession, yet in reality he is always there first. What our intercession achieves is that his power, his love and his faithfulness are shown ever more clearly in the midst of the people. (Pope Francis, *Evangelii Gaudium* 283)

One story from Scripture which shows the power of communal prayer is from the Book of Acts, when Peter is arrested and imprisoned by King Herod who, ordered "four squads of four soldiers each to guard him in turns" (*Ac* 12:4). The Word of God tells us that, "All the time Peter was under guard the Church prayed to God for him unremittingly" (v. 5), and then we read about Peter's miraculous release by an angel of the Lord!

In his encyclical *Evangelii Gaudium* Pope Francis encourages us to reach out to people in their everyday lives and pray with them about their concerns (cf. 127, 128). I remember the first time that occurred in my own life, when, many years ago, I ran into a young woman whom I had met briefly through a mutual friend. I had heard that she had just been diagnosed with cervical cancer, and knew that she had two small children. I also knew she was a lapsed Catholic. While we were speaking I felt a strong inner prompting to pray with her - which I strongly resisted. This young woman was highly intelligent and stunningly beautiful: rather intimidating to say the least. Also, I was a rather 'private' Catholic and would rather just have prayed for her later at home, or even at Mass. But eventually I obeyed the prompting and asked her if she would like to pray. She gripped my arm and whispered yes. As I prayed she wept and we experienced exactly what Jesus said: "Where two or three meet in my name I shall be there with them" (*Mt* 18:20). Since then I have not hesitated to pray with others and give the Lord the opportunity he is looking for to bless them with his love.

Praying takes us out of our selves: it widens our horizons and expands our hearts, removing our gaze from self-concern. Private prayer helps us deepen our relationship with God: it is 'conversation with God'. We don't always have to use words - sometimes sighs and tears are enough, as long as we have turned our heart and mind to him.

This spiritual work of mercy, like all the others, is geared towards "*the greatest gift of mercy*: bringing people to Christ and giving them the opportunity to know and savour his love" (St John Paul II).

Mercy Works

Mark P. Shea

The spiritual and corporal works of mercy are not a list to be learnt but actions to be lived. Mark Shea gives great examples of people who have performed the works of mercy and advice on how we can practise them in the 21st century. Pope Francis's Year of Mercy is a call to each one of us to rediscover and to live the works of mercy every day.

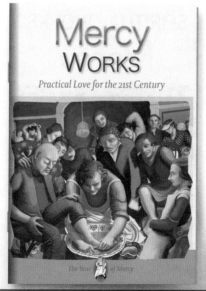

PA25   ISBN 978 1 78469 076 2

Spiritual Works of Mercy

Mgr Paul Grogan

Most Christians want to live an active faith yet feel perplexed about how to do so. The seven interconnected 'spiritual works of mercy' come to our aid: counselling the doubtful; instructing the ignorant; admonishing sinners; comforting the afflicted; forgiving offences; bearing wrongs patiently; and praying for the living and the dead. Through such acts of mercy we can respond fully to God's goodness towards us, involving conversion of our interior life: such acts are truly God's acts of mercy; we, mere human agents for God to alleviate people's unhappiness.

SP46   ISBN 978 1 78469 087 8

Corporal Works of Mercy
Mercy in Action
Mgr Richard Atherton

Feeding the hungry and thirsty, clothing the naked, housing the homeless, visiting the imprisoned, visiting the sick, and burying the dead - Pope Francis wants us to stop and think again, especially during the Year of Mercy. Are these things I can do, or are they for others to get on with? What good do they do? Actions of mercy are often terribly ordinary and doable. Mgr Atherton guides us through the spiritual and practical matters that Love asks of all Christians.

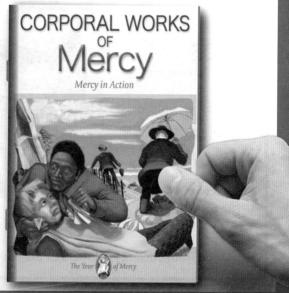

SP45 ISBN: 978 1 78469 080 9